Using To

GW00738318

Contents

A hairdresser's tools

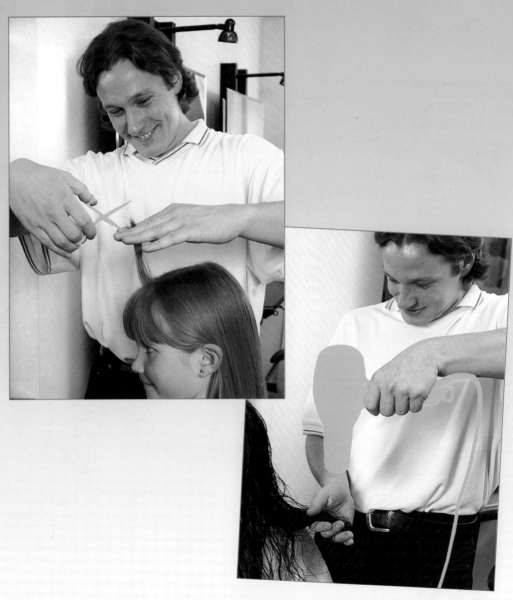

A hairdresser uses many tools.

comb

scissors

hair dryer

Which tools is he using?

3

A gardener's tools

A gardener uses many tools.

shears

rake

spade

Which tools is she using?

A chef's tools

A chef uses many tools.

grater

mixing bowl

rolling pin

Which tools is he using?

A doctor's tools

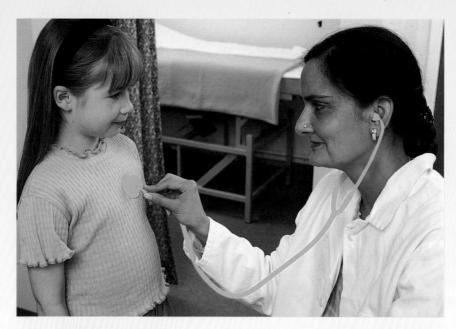

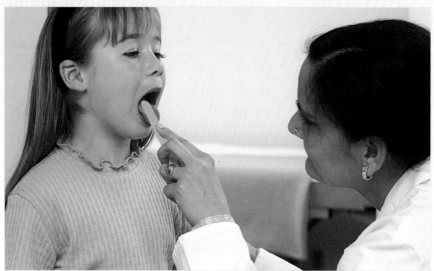

A doctor uses many tools.

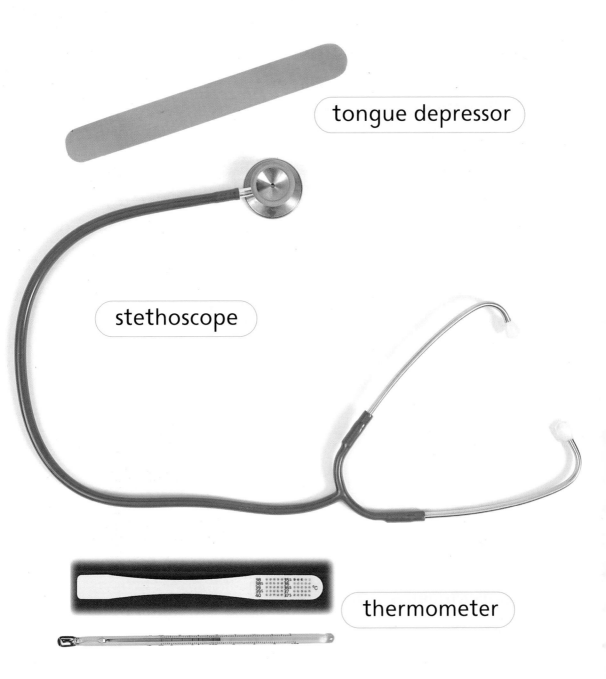

tongue depressor

stethoscope

thermometer

Which tools is she using?

A carpenter's tools

A carpenter uses many tools.

drill

hammer

saw

Which tools is he using?

A vet's tools

A vet uses many tools.

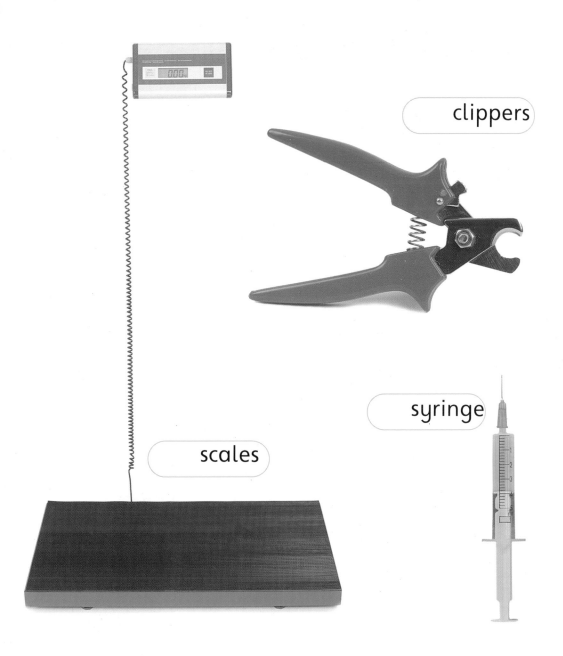

clippers

syringe

scales

Which tools is she using?

Which tools are they using?

Hairdresser

Gardener

Chef

Doctor

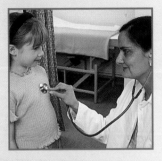  

Carpenter

Vet

Index

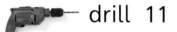
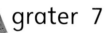
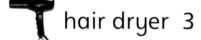
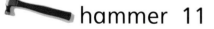
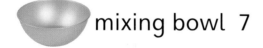
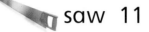